PORSCHE

INTRO

Dass CURVES eine Leidenschaft für Südostasien pflegt, haben wir mit unserer großen Thailand-Ausgabe bereits verraten. Und mit dem hier vorliegenden Sneak-In-CURVES wollen wir erneut nach Asien reisen, unser Ziel ist Malaysia. Wir mögen den bunten Strudel des Lebens, die Vielfalt und Exotik der Kulturen Südostasiens, die Freundlichkeit der Menschen, das Essen und die Landschaften. Wer aber dachte, dass dieses Land nur aus wunderschönen Stränden, turbulenten Städten und dichtem Dschungel besteht, muss sich eines Besseren belehren lassen: Auf den Inseln und Halbinseln zwischen Indischem Ozean und Pazifischem Ozean kann man ganz ausgezeichnet Auto fahren, auch für uns ist das nach wie vor eine echte Überraschung. Kurvige Straßen führen bis hinauf in die Gebirge des Landesinneren oder palmenbesäumt entlang der Küsten, wirbeln als wenig befahrene und häufig gut ausgebaute Fahrspaß-Jäger durchs Land. Damit dieser Geheimtipp auch wirklich unser (und nun auch Ihr ...) süßes Geheimnis bleibt, haben wir die hier vorliegende Ausgabe in streng limitierter Auflage gestaltet: CURVES Malaysia möchte Sie mit auf die Reise in den Dschungel nehmen, in ein magisches Paralleluniversum des 330.000 Quadratkilometer großen Landes zwischen Singapur und Thailand. Als kleines Guckloch in eine völlig andere Welt. Schnallen Sie sich also fest, öffnen Sie alle Sinne, starten Sie die Motoren. Kommen Sie von der Hauptstadt Kuala Lumpur aus mit auf zwei Loops zwischen der Ostküste und Westküste Malaysias – rund 1.600 Kilometer nach Norden und knapp 1.000 Kilometer nach Süden. Hinein in eine Welt aus saftigem Grün, triefnassem Urwald, fremden Kulturen, Abenteuern und Erlebnissen. *Soulful Driving in Malaysia.*

The fact that CURVES has a passion for Southeast Asia was something we revealed in our big Thailand issue. This sneak-in edition of CURVES sees a return to Asia. Our destination this time? Malaysia. We love the colorful, confused whirligig of life here, the diversity and exoticism of Southeast Asia's cultures, the friendliness of the people, the food and the landscapes. But if you thought this country was just about beautiful beaches, bustling cities and dense jungle, you need to think again: the islands and peninsulas between the Indian and Pacific Oceans are a great place to drive a car, something that was a genuine surprise, even for us. Winding roads lead up into the mountains of the country's interior or cling to the coast lined with palm trees. These little-used and often well-built thoroughfares thread their way through the country, offering plenty of pleasure for drivers.

To ensure that this insider tip really does remain our (and now also your...) sweet little secret, we have decided to make this a strictly limited edition: CURVES Malaysia is going to take you on a journey into the jungle, to a magical parallel universe in the 330,000 square kilometer country between Singapore and Thailand. We will offer you a chance to peep into a completely different world. So... buckle up, sharpen all of your senses and start your engines. Setting out from the capital Kuala Lumpur, join us on two loops between the east coast and west coast of Malaysia, travelling around 1,600 kilometers to the north and almost 1,000 kilometers to the south. Enter a world of lush green, dripping wet jungle, fascinating cultures, adventures and experiences. *Soulful Driving in Malaysia.*

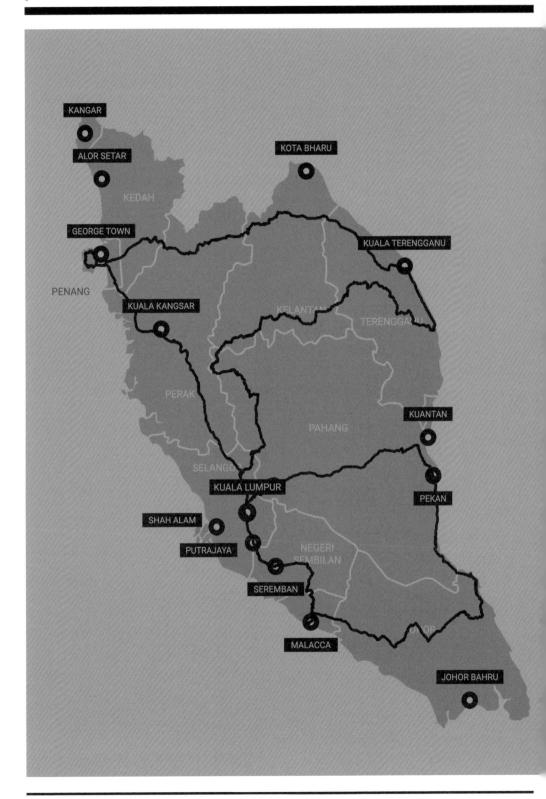

EDI
TOR
IAL

In Kuala Lumpur beginnt alles. „KL" ist nicht nur die Hauptstadt des multikulturellen Staats Malaysia, sondern auch ein Portal in seine bunte Welt. Die Stadt ist ein erster Schock für unser System, ein gut gezielter Handkantenschlag ins Genick unserer gleichförmigen Fortbewegung. Hallo! Aufwachen! – „Kuala Lumpur" bedeutet in etwa so viel wie „die Mündung eines schlammigen Flusses", aber dieses uralte Delta der Flüsse Klang und Gombak ist längst unter dem Brodeln der Millionenstadt untergegangen. Das sich schüchtern dahinziehende Netz kleiner Kanäle im Bild der Stadt erweckt kaum noch den Eindruck, einmal Namensgeber oder gar Anziehungspunkt für die ersten Siedler gewesen sein zu können. Bergarbeiter, die sich auf der Suche nach Zinn in die Berge wühlten und dann Mitte der 1800er-Jahre Kuala Lumpur mitten im Urwald gründeten.

Heute ist die Stadt ein Riese – und sie wächst unaufhörlich. Gigantische Wolkenkratzer recken sich grauen Wolken entgegen, die schwülheiße Luft ist gesättigt mit Feuchtigkeit. Bei Nacht bestürmen Myriaden von Lichtern den Dunst der Tropen, die blinkenden Türme stehen wie die Bauten von Riesenglühwürmchen in der Ebene, während tropische Gewitter Blitze aus dunklen Wolkentürmen schleudern. Darunter verschlingen Häuserfluten einen ganzen Landstrich. Und auch wenn das alles ein klein wenig apokalyptisch klingt, ist Kuala Lumpur eine freundliche Stadt. Grün und lebendig, vielfältig, leuchtend, aufregend. Ihre Kolonialvergangenheit lebt in stei-

Our story begins in Kuala Lumpur. "KL" is not just the capital of the multicultural state of Malaysia, but also the gateway to its colorful world. The city is a shock to our system at first, a well-aimed smack to the back of the head to rouse us from our monotonous driving habits. Hi there! Time to wake up! – "Kuala Lumpur" means something like "the mouth of a muddy river", but this ancient delta of the rivers Klang and Gombak has long since disappeared under the heaving metropolis we now see before us. It is hard to believe from the shyly meandering network of little canals dotted around the city that there was once a mighty confluence here that attracted the first settlers. These were miners who ventured into the mountains in search of tin and then founded Kuala Lumpur in the middle of the jungle in the mid-1800s.

Today the city has grown to gigantic proportions and continues to spread. Huge skyscrapers stretch towards gray clouds and the muggy air is saturated with moisture. At night, myriad lights break through the tropical haze and the twinkling towers stand like structures built by giant fireflies on the plains, while tropical thunderstorms hurl bolts of lightning from darkly towering clouds. Down below, thousands of houses engulf an entire region. While this all sounds a little apocalyptic, Kuala Lumpur is actually a friendly city – green and lively, multifaceted, luminous and thrilling. The city's colonial past lives on in its stone palaces, mighty colosses with baroque

nernen Palästen fort, mächtigen Kolossen mit barocken Fassaden, an denen sich grauer Pilzbelag in die Winkel und Ritzen der Erker frisst. Geschäfte und Läden, Imbissstände und Marktbuden ducken sich in den Schatten bunter Zeltplanen. Lampions in allen Farben schaukeln an Bändern in kleinen Gassen, ziehen Motten an und Licht und Menschen. Pulks von Mopedfahrern schmettern als atmende Schwarmintelligenz auf die Sperrflächen an Ampeln, diese heimlichen Herrscher des Straßenverkehrs von Kuala Lumpur fluten dann knatternd die mehrspurigen Boulevards. Blaugrau spiegelnde Glasfassaden stürzen aus dem Himmel herab und zerschellen in Grünanlagen, Baukräne schlingern auf Skyscraper-Sockeln und in der Ferne branden Hügelketten gegen die Stadt, bedeckt mit dichtem, grünem Pelz aus Dschungel.

Hier fahren wir also los, lassen Kuala Lumpur hinter uns. Fließen hinaus, während die Stadt langsam ihren festen Griff lockert, besteigen die ersten Berge. Tempel wuchern im Dschungel, mit Pagoden-Dächern, auf denen Drachen balancieren, während sie grässliche, lautlose Schreie ausstoßen. Schwärme von Göttern und Gestalten kauern in bunte Gewänder gehüllt auf den Simsen, wispern hypnotische Sätze, recken beschwörende Hände, schwenken Elefantenrüssel, schließen andächtige Fingerspitzen. Kerzen flackern ewig in Betten aus Sand und Asche, beleuchten die Gaben der Gläubigen. Götterstatuen hüten Felsengrotten, über und über mit Gold bedeckt, stoisch ins Jenseits schauend, Weisheiten bewahrend. Dabei sind diese Wesenheiten nur geduldet, herübergewandert aus Indien und China – die Staatsreligion Malaysias ist aber der Islam. Und der kennt

facades where gray-colored lichen eats into the corners and cracks of the bay windows. There are serried ranks of shops, food stands and market stalls in the shadows of colorful tarpaulin covers. Lanterns in every imaginable color bob and sway on ribbons in narrow alleys, attracting moths and lighting the way for passers-by. Like single, breathing, intelligent entities, flocks of moped drivers draw to a sudden halt at traffic lights before flooding onto the multi-lane boulevards with a clatter – the secret rulers of Kuala Lumpur's roads. Blue-gray reflecting glass facades seem to drop from the sky, driving themselves deep into green areas, while construction cranes lurch on their skyscraper perches and, in the distance, chains of hills covered with dense, green jungle vegetation surge towards the city. This is our starting point, the place where we leave Kuala Lumpur behind.

We follow the flow of traffic as the city slowly loosens its grip, climbing our first mountains. Temples sprawl in the jungle, their pagoda-roofs providing a place for dragons to perform a balancing act, all the while uttering ghastly, silent screams. Hosts of deities and other figures, swathed in colorful robes, crouch on temple ledges, whispering hypnotic incantations, stretching out imploring hands, waving elephant trunks, closing their fingertips in elegant reverence. Candles flicker eternally in beds of sand and ash, illuminating the offerings of the faithful.

Statues of gods preside over gilded rock grottos, stoically gazing into the afterlife, guardians of preserved wisdom. Having wandered in from India and China, these

ROAD TO GENTING HIGHLANDS

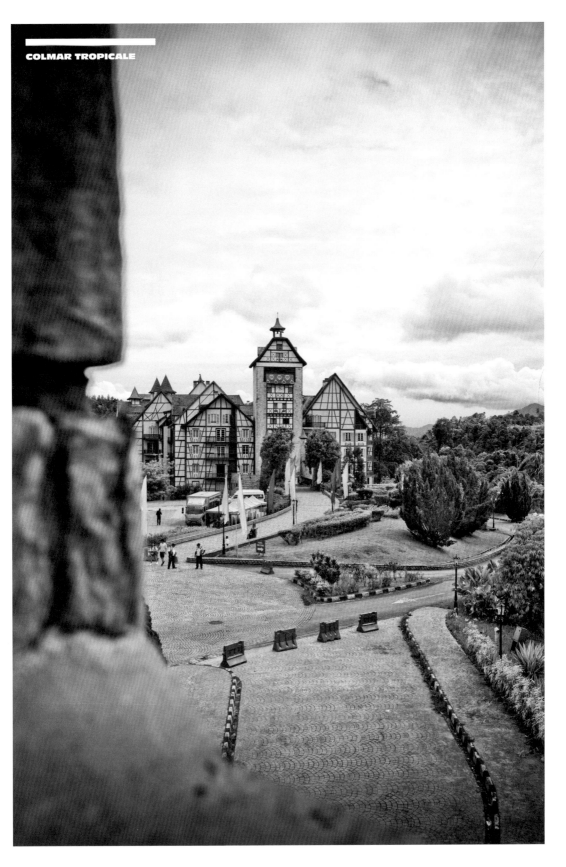

keine Bildnisse von Gottheiten, keinen Rausch der Kreaturen, die Bildsprache des Islam ist rein ornamental. Das Gebet nehmen die Malaien ernst, fünfmal am Tag, es gibt kleine Kompasse auf Reise-Gebetsteppichen, damit man sich bei der Andacht auch wirklich in Richtung Mekka neigt, Nordwesten von hier aus. Unten am Indischen Ozean ziehen derweil lehmbraune Mahlströme durch Mangroven, tunkt der Urwald vorsichtig seine Füße an hellen Sandstränden ins Wasser. Palmen schwenken wedelnde Kronen in den Gezeiten des Windes, Wellen schwappen über Felsen, füllen Tümpel, tränken Algengärten. Aber wir haben all dem den Rücken zugedreht und suchen kühle Berghöhen. Auf den Dünndarmschlingen der Serpentinenstraße surfen wir in die Hänge, während Tee-Plantagen auf den zerfurchten Flanken nisten und erzürnte Urwald-Riesen daneben mit Flechten bewachsene Häupter schütteln. Die Straße wirft sich in den Wald, hetzt bereits jetzt schon atemlos dahin, hat Fährte aufgenommen. Gierig hechelnd fetzt sie ins Grün, scheucht faule Affen mit lässiger Geste von sich. Bröckelnde Brücken hüpfen über Bäche, Betonplanken nehmen den Asphalt an Engstellen in die Klemme: Super Mario, Turbo-Boost-Jump.

Bambus greift nach uns, Schlingpflanzen werfen zuschnappende Lassos, Baumriesen wachen aus trägem Dahindösen auf. Die Welt trieft und tropft, der Asphalt wirbelt als

beings are benignly tolerated, as the state religion of Malaysia is Islam. The Koran does not permit images of deities, or other fabulous creatures – the visual language of Islam is purely ornamental. The Malays take prayer very seriously, stopping work for religious observance five times a day. There are even tiny compasses on travel prayer mats so that you really do face towards Mecca, northwest of here, when praying.

Meanwhile, down by the Indian Ocean, clay-brown maelstroms cut through the mangroves, and the jungle gingerly dips its feet in the water on the light-colored sandy beaches. Palm trees wave their fronded crowns in the wind, while the waves slap over rocks, filling pools and irrigating gardens of seaweed. But we turn our backs on all that, seeking out the cool mountain heights. We surf the hillsides on the twisting loops of the narrow serpentine road, while tea plantations nestle on the rugged flanks and craggy jungle giants shake their lichen-covered heads in anger. The road flings itself impetuously into the forest, already rushing along breathlessly like a bloodhound, scattering sleepy monkeys with a casual gesture. We bounce our way over streams on crumbling bridges. Concrete stanchions rein in the asphalt at bottlenecks: it feels like we're playing Super Mario, Turbo Boost Jump.

nasses Band ins Grün des Urwalds. Jemand hat das Autoradio an, Axl Rose knarzt „Welcome to the Jungle" und Slash wetzt an den Röhren seines Marshall-Amps das Sägemesser seiner Les Paul dazu ... Dann haben wir die ersten Kuppen erreicht und schauen ins Weite. Sehen grauweiße Wolkengruppen über einen blassblauen Himmel segeln, Terrassen in den Hängen und darunter neue Städte, wie ein Pilz, dessen Myzel einen ganzen Horizont untergraben kann. Durch monotone Palmölplantagen ziehen wir nun schnurgerade dahin, schauen zu, wie Bäume im Gleichschritt-Marsch an uns vorüberziehen, gelangweilt und grübelnd.

Das bunte Wirbeln der Städte ist auf dieser Reise immer wieder unser Ziel, wie Süchtige streben wir schnüffelnd auf die Märkte und in die Gassen mit den Garküchen. Fleisch und Gemüse auf Spießen wartet dort in ganzen Pyramiden, bis sie in Öl und Fett baden dürfen, in Sambal-Soßen getunkt werden, gekocht und gedünstet sind. In Bananenblätter gehüllte Fische braten auf gusseisernen Platten, werden dabei aber auch immer wieder mit Wasser oder Sojasauce benetzt und so nebenbei gedünstet. Gekochter Reis wartet in mächtigen Schalen auf hungrige Esser, man serviert ihn in Schalen, fasst ihn mit triefenden Fingern und führt ihn zusammen mit Stücken von Fleisch oder Gemüse und getränkt mit Soßen zum Mund. Malaysia schmeckt nach Indien und China

Fingers of bamboo seem to reach out to grab us, creepers form snapping lassos and giant trees wake from a lazy slumber. This is a world full of drips and drops. The asphalt twists through the green of the jungle like a wet silken ribbon. Someone has switched the car radio on in time for us to hear Axl Rose croak "Welcome to the Jungle" while Slash sharpens his Les Paul axe on his Marshall amp... By then we have reached the first peaks and peer into the distance. Clusters of gray-white clouds sail across a pale blue sky. The slopes are scored with terraces and new cities appear below, like a fungus whose mycelium can erode an entire horizon. We now move forward in a dead straight line through monotonous palm oil plantations, watching as trees march past us in step, bored and brooding.

The colorful hurly-burly of the cities is our constant goal on this trip. We are like addicts as we sniff out the markets and the alley kitchens. Whole pyramids of meat and vegetables on skewers wait there to be bathed in oil and fat, dipped in sambal sauces, boiled and stewed. Fish wrapped in banana leaves roast on cast-iron griddles, but are also repeatedly moistened with water or soy sauce and steamed in the process. Boiled rice awaits hungry stomachs in huge cauldrons. It is served in bowls, picked up with dripping fingers, drenched with sauce and stuffed into your mouth together with

GEORGE TOWN

Glücklich und mit Curry-tropfenden Fingern sitzt man dann nach einem reichhaltigen Dinner auf den obligatorischen Plastikstühlen der Streetfood-Läden, schaut sich um, nimmt das Lärmen der Musik, das Plappern und Lachen der Menschen umso intensiver auf.

Happily sated after a sumptuous dinner, our fingers dripping with curry, we sit on the obligatory plastic chairs in the street food shops, looking around, absorbing the noise of the music and the chattering and laughing of the people all the more intensively.

zugleich, kennt Einflüsse Arabiens ebenso wie Andeutungen europäischer Küche. Nudeln treffen auf Reis, Hühnchen auf Meeresfrüchte, Suppen auf Gegrilltes, scharfe Chili und Ingwer auf süß und exotisch schmeckende Früchte. Alkohol ist aus religiösen Gründen kein großes Thema, dafür lieben Malaien Drinks aus Säften und Eis, bunte Smoothies und opulente Mixgetränke. Natürlich gehört zur Reise durch Malaysia eine Bucket-List an Gerichten, die man für ein kulinarisches 360-Grad-Erlebnis unbedingt abhaken sollte. Beginnend mit dem Nationalgericht Nasi Lemak, einer sonderbaren Mischung aus Kokosreis, Spiegelei, Hühnchen und getrockneten Fischchen.

Auch die sogenannten Roti, indische Fladenbrote oder Pfannkuchen, gehören zu Malaysia, werden mit scharfen Soßen, Dips, in Suppen und Brühen oder auch mit süßen Zutaten gereicht. Die Kokos-Chili-Suppe Laksa sorgt dann wieder für pikante Schärfe,

morsels of meat or vegetables. Malaysia tastes like a mixture of India and China, with influences from Arabia as well as hints of European cuisine. Noodles rub shoulders with rice, chicken mixes with seafood, soups meet grilled dishes, hot chili and ginger mingle with sweet and exotic fruits. Alcohol is not big here for religious reasons, but the Malays love drinks made from juice and ice, colorful smoothies and opulent mixed drinks.

Of course, a trip through Malaysia includes a number of dishes that you should definitely check off your bucket list for a complete culinary experience. These start with the national dish, nasi lemak, an odd mix of coconut rice, fried egg, chicken and dried fish. So-called roti, Indian flatbreads or pancakes, are also part of Malaysian cuisine and are served with hot sauces, dips, in soups and broths or with sweet ingredients. The coconut-chili soup

Bratnudeln Mee Goreng oder Nasi Ayam-Hühnchenreis für hohe Umami-Dosen, zum Nachtisch gibt es Cendol: aus Shaved Ice, Kokosmilch, Reismehl-Nudeln, Palmzucker und – wilde Kombi – roten Bohnen. Glücklich und mit Curry-tropfenden Fingern sitzt man dann nach einem reichhaltigen Dinner auf den obligatorischen Plastikstühlen der Streetfood-Läden, schaut sich um, nimmt das Lärmen der Musik, das Plappern und Lachen der Menschen umso intensiver auf. Lauscht dem kehligen-rollenden Dialekt des Malaiischen, studiert die Gesichter. – Malaysia ist ein Land vieler Kulturen, die Lage an den Haupt-Handelsrouten zwischen Europa und Asien, Indien und China hat das Land stark geprägt. Etwas mehr als die Hälfte der heutigen Malaien entstammen den ursprünglichen Bewohnern der Malaiischen Halbinsel und der Insel Borneo, rund ein Viertel der Einwohner sind Chinesen, knapp 10 Prozent haben indische Vorfahren. Nach einer bewegten Geschichte waren es die europäischen Kolonialnationen Portugal, Holland und England, die sich in ihrem Streben nach globaler Macht den Regionen des heutigen Malaysias bemächtigten und ihnen ihren Stempel aufdrückten. Dass Malaysia bis zu seiner Unabhängigkeit 1963 aus vier Teilen des britischen Empires bestand, ist der Kultur auch heute noch ein klein wenig abzuspüren: Englisch wird in Malaysia gut und häufig gesprochen, die politische Kultur und viele Werte sind trotz einer Verwurzelung der Malaien in südostasiatischen Kulturen und im Islam europäisch angehaucht.

Typisch Malaiisch ist also, dass es so etwas wie „typisch malaiisch" nicht gibt – höchstens vielleicht eine Partie „Sepak Takraw". Diese Mischung aus Badminton und Fußball, bei der eine Art Kunststoff-Rattanball im superflexiblen Kickbox-Stil über ein Netz getreten wird, ist nur in Malaysia zu Hause.

laksa then provides spicy heat again, fried noodles mee goreng or nasi ayam chicken rice for high doses of umami. For dessert there is cendol: made of shaved ice, coconut milk, rice flour noodles, palm sugar and – a wild combination – red beans. Happily sated after a sumptuous dinner, our fingers dripping with curry, we sit on the obligatory plastic chairs in the street food shops, looking around, absorbing the noise of the music and the chattering and laughing of the people all the more intensively. We listen to the throaty, rolling dialect of Malay and study the faces around us. – Malaysia is a country of many cultures, the location on the main trade routes between Europe and Asia, India and China has strongly influenced the country.

A little more than half of today's Malays come from the original inhabitants of the Malay Peninsula and the island of Borneo. Around a quarter of the inhabitants are Chinese, almost 10 percent have Indian ancestry. After an eventful history, it was the European colonial nations of Portugal, Holland and England who, in their quest for global power, seized the regions of present-day Malaysia and left their mark on them. The fact that Malaysia consisted of four parts of the British Empire until it gained independence in 1963 is still evident in its culture today: English is spoken well and frequently in Malaysia, the political culture and many values still have a European character, despite the Malays being rooted in Southeast Asian cultures and in Islam.

Typically for Malaysia, there is no such thing as "typically Malaysian" – at most maybe a game of "Sepak Takraw". This mix of badminton and soccer, which involves kicking a type of plastic rattan ball over a net in a super-flexible kickboxing style, is unique to Malaysia.

UP TO FRASER'S HILL

SUNGAI KOYAN

FRASER'S HILL

THE NORTH LOOP

Kuala Lumpur frisst sich wie eine Häuser-Lawine in die Ebene zwischen Küste und Bergen, im Norden der malaiischen Hauptstadt ragt ein erster Emissär der umgebenden Hügelketten aus dem urbanen Dickicht: schroffe Kalkstein-Knoten inmitten der Häuser, mit senkrecht abfallenden Felswänden und von Bäumen bedeckten Häuptern. Und im Bauch dieser Ungetüme verbergen sich tiefe Höhlen, Wohnort von Lebewesen die Dunkelheit mögen, Sitz uralter Hindu-Gottheiten. Die Batu-Höhlen sind unser erster Stopp auf der Reise über den Norden der Malaiischen Halbinsel. Von hier aus geht es nun endgültig über die Stadtgrenzen hinaus, die kleine Straße 68 windet sich eine Zeit lang parallel der sechsspurigen Schnellstraße E8 nach Nordosten. Tapfer stürmt sie in die Berge, lässt die letzten Ausläufer der Hauptstadt zurück, schon bald wird es hier oben einsam. Die Berge übernehmen, Geisterhäuser, Tempel und Schreine begleiten uns ins Genting Hochland und die letzten Kilometer sind nur über eine wahre Serpentinen-Achterbahn zu erreichen. Malaysias „Col de Turini" nennen Insider dieses Kurvenmonster zum Erlebnispark auf einem Berggipfel.

Und weil sie so schön waren, die ersten Kurven Malaysias, trudeln wir die Straße auch gleich wieder hinunter. Zurück ins Tal und dann auf der B66 weiter nach Norden. Über Batang Kali und Rasa bis Kuala Kubu, dann hinter dem Sungai-Selangor-Staudamm ins Gebirge hinein. Was jetzt kommt, scheint den Träumen aller Sportwagen- und Motorradfahrer entstiegen: eine Strecke, die sich

Kuala Lumpur eats its way into the plain between the mountains and the coast like an architectural avalanche. In the north of the Malaysian capital, the first outliers of the surrounding hills rise from the urban sprawl: rugged limestone crags squeeze between the buildings, with vertical cliffs and tree-covered peaks. In the bellies of these monsters are deep caverns, the dwelling place of beings that prefer to live in darkness, the seat of ancient Hindu deities. The Batu Caves are our first stop on the journey across the north of Peninsular Malaysia.

From here we finally escape the city limits and the small route 68 runs parallel to the six-lane E8 expressway to the northeast for a while. It then bravely storms into the mountains, leaving the last foothills of the capital behind. Things will get lonely up here soon. The mountains take over, spirit houses, temples and shrines accompany our journey into the Genting Highlands and the last few kilometers are a veritable serpentine roller coaster. Insiders refer to this monster set of curves as Malaysia's "Col de Turini", an adventure park on a mountain peak.

Because the first bends in Malaysia were so beautiful, we continue on down the road right away, returning to the valley and then journeying further north on the B66. We travel via Batang Kali and Rasa to Kuala Kubu, then beyond the Sungai Selangor Dam into the mountains. What we now

verbissen und lustvoll kurvend als grüner Tunnel durch einen dichten Dschungel schraubt, rock 'n' rollend, heftig groovend, schwindlig, wahnsinnig, unaufhörlich. Rund um den Fraser's Hill, hinüber nach Raub – und erst dort beruhigt sich der ekstatische Puls dieser Straße. Surft bis Sungai Koyan und schlägt dann hinüber in die Cameron Highlands wieder eine etwas lebendigere Gangart an, ohne jedoch den vorherigen Kurven-Irrwitz wieder zu entfachen.

In den Hochtälern hier oben wird Tee angebaut, sanftgrüne Terrassen rollen aus von Dunst umwaberten Berghängen herab, die Straße folgt dieser Welt eine Zeit lang, schaut sich neugierig um und verschwindet dann endgültig wieder im Dschungel. Scheinbar endlos breitet der sich in alle Himmelsrichtungen aus, ein Geheimnis aus Grün in tausenden Schattierungen. Weiter, weiter, immer weiter – beinahe hypnotisiert fahren wir dahin. Bis zum Tasik Kenyir, einem riesenhaften Seengebiet, das mit seinen schwarzgrünen Gewässer-Armen und bewaldeten Inseln eine enorme Fläche einnimmt. Elefanten sollen hier oben leben, zwischen Wald und Wasser. Während wir auf der Straße weiterfahren, halten wir die ganze Zeit Ausschau nach den Dickhäutern, die sich heute aber im Unterholz verbergen. Langsam, ganz langsam nähern wir uns nun der östlichen Seite der malaiischen Halbinsel, am Golf von Thailand. Bis Kuala Dungun fahren wir, der kleinen Stadt an der Mündung des Sungai Dungun. Nach Kurven und Wald steht uns nun ein krasser Szenenwechsel bevor: Rund 70 Kilometer weit sind wir nun bis ins große Kuala Terengganu entlang der Küste unterwegs. Kerzengerade zieht die AH18 dahin, als vielbefahrene Palmen-Allee, wir streifen Terengganu im Westen, schon zieht es uns wieder ins Landesinnere. Die dicht

encounter is something from the dreams of all sports car drivers and motorbike riders: a track that twists doggedly and joyfully as a green tunnel through dense jungle. This is a madly dizzying, never-ending, truly grooving rock 'n' roll experience. We swing around Fraser's Hill and cross to Raub, where the ecstatic pulse of this road finally calms down. We surf our way up to Sungai Koyan and then pick up a slightly livelier pace as we cross into the Cameron Highlands, but without returning to the previous crazy curves.

Tea is cultivated in the high valleys up here, where soft green terraces roll down from misty mountain slopes. The road follows this world for a while, looking around in curiosity before finally disappearing back into the jungle. A seemingly endless green mystery in thousands of shades spreads out in every direction. We drive onward, ever onward, almost hypnotized. Finally we reach Tasik Kenyir, a huge lake district that occupies an enormous area with its black-green fingers of water and densely forested islands. Elephants are rumored to live up here, between the forest and the water. As we continue along the road, we keep a sharp lookout for the pachyderms, but they are obviously hiding in the undergrowth today. Slowly, very slowly, we are now nearing the eastern side of the Malay Peninsula and the Gulf of Thailand.

We drive to Kuala Dungun, the small town at the mouth of the Sungai Dungun. After a landscape of curves and forest, we are now faced with an eye-popping change of scenery: we find ourselves travelling about 70 kilometers along the coast to the big city of Kuala Terengganu. The AH18 is straight as an arrow, a busy palm tree-lined avenue. We pass Terengganu in the west and are already drawn inland again. The densely

In den Hochtälern hier oben wird Tee angebaut, sanftgrüne Terrassen rollen aus von Dunst umwaberten
Berghängen herab, die Straße folgt dieser Welt eine
Zeit lang, schaut sich neugierig um und verschwindet
dann endgültig wieder im Dschungel. Scheinbar endlos breitet der sich in alle Himmelsrichtungen aus, ein
Geheimnis aus Grün in tausenden Schattierungen.

Tea is cultivated in the high valleys up here, where soft
green terraces roll down from misty mountain slopes.
The road follows this world for a while, looking around
in curiosity before finally disappearing back into the
jungle. A seemingly endless green mystery in thousands
of shades spreads out in every direction.

besiedelten Küstengebiete mit ihren raum-
greifenden Geraden üben auf uns eben
nur wenig Anziehungskraft aus, wir wollen
zurück in die Wildnis. Schneiden deshalb
weit südlich von Kelantan an der Grenze
nach Thailand in Richtung Westen, zielen
mit der gelassen durchs Land schwingenden „Lebuhraya Timur-Barat 4" über die
gesamte Halbinsel von Ost nach West. Aus
dem Bundesstaat Perak geht es nach Kedah,
bei Kulim in den Bundesstaat Penang – und
hier sind wir nach rund 450 Kilometern
quer durch das Land wieder am Indischen
Ozean angekommen, der Straße von Malakka zwischen Malaysia und der indonesi-
schen Insel Sumatra.

Erneut füllt sich die flache Küstenebene mit
Häusern, Fabriken, Industriekomplexen,
ineinander wuchernden Stadtgebieten. Südlich von Butterworth strebt hier die E36 auf
den flachen Pfeilern des Jambatan-Pulau-
Pinang-Brückenkomplexes über eine rund

populated coastal areas with their endless straight lines have little to attract us
and we yearn to return to the wilderness.
Hence, far south of Kelantan on the border
with Thailand, we cut off in a westerly direction, heading across the entire peninsula from east to west on the "Lebuhraya
Timur-Barat 4", which winds serenely
through the countryside. Emerging from
the state of Perak we drive to Kedah, enter-
ing the state of Penang near Kulim. Here,
after travelling about 450 kilometers across
the country, we have arrived back at the
Indian Ocean, the Strait of Malacca between Malaysia and the Indonesian island
of Sumatra.

The flat coastal plain is once again filled
with houses, factories, industrial com-
plexes and urban areas that spread into
one another. South of Butterworth, the
E36 crosses a 13 km wide strait on the stur-
dy pillars of the Jambatan-Pulau-Pinang

13 Kilometer breite Meerenge und landet dann auf der Insel Penang. Deren große Stadt George Town ist ein wahres Mekka für Streetfood-Obsessive, Feinschmecker und andere Verfressene, die Insel selbst mit der Rundstraße Nummer 6 eine kleine Rundfahrt wert: Von George Town fahren wir an die Nordspitze Penangs bei Batu Ferringhi, nehmen dann hinter Teluk Bahang die kurvenreiche Straße direkt ans südliche Ende der Insel bei Teluk Kumbar und fahren dann zurück ans Festland. Vorbei an der alten malaiischen Stadt Taiping und Ipoh, der Hauptstadt des Bundesstaats Perak, geht es nun wieder zurück nach Süden.

Viele Kilometer weit streift die Straße dahin. Zur Rechten, im Osten, verfolgen uns die Berge zwischen Perak und dem Bundesstaat Pahang, zur Linken breitet sich eine Landschaft aus, in der schlammige, mäandernde Flüsse in Richtung Ozean streben. Viele Quadratkilometer sind mit Palmöl-Plantagen bedeckt, die Wedel der Pflanzungen ziehen sich als monotone Einöden bis an den Horizont. Von hier also kommen die Millionen Liter Palmöl, die Malaysia zusammen mit dem Nachbarn Indonesien auf den Weltmarkt drückt. Südlich der Grenze zum Bundesstaat Selangor darf das Land wieder aufatmen, hier breitet sich der Raja-Musa-Regenwald aus, ein Labyrinth aus Sümpfen und undurchdringlichem Dickicht. Bevor wir die Hauptstadt Kuala Lumpur und mit ihr das Ziel unserer Etappe erreichen, muss aber noch ein letzter Abstecher über die Berge sein: Statt dem bequemen Schlenker im Tal, über Rawang, wählen wir die B23 durch den Selangor State Park. Ein letztes Mal Kurven im Urwald, dann hat uns die Großstadt wieder.

bridge complex and finally ends up on the island of Penang. The large city of George Town is a genuine magnet for street food fans, gourmets and other foodies, and the island itself is worth a short tour on circular road number 6. From George Town we drive to the northern tip of Penang at Batu Ferringhi, then take the winding road beyond Teluk Bahang Road straight to the southern end of the island at Teluk Kumbar and then return to the mainland. Passing the old Malay city of Taiping and Ipoh, the capital of the state of Perak, we now head back south.

The road stretches ahead for many kilometers. To the right, to the east, the mountains between Perak and Pahang state follow us in hot pursuit. To the left, a landscape of muddy, meandering rivers push toward the ocean. Many square kilometers are covered with palm oil plantations, the waving fronds of the plantations stretch to the horizon like monotonous wastelands. This is where the millions of liters of palm oil that Malaysia and its neighbor Indonesia push onto the world market come from. South of the border with the state of Selangor, the country starts to breathe again. Here the Raja Musa rainforest spreads itself in a labyrinth of swamps and impenetrable thickets. Before we reach the capital Kuala Lumpur and the end of this stage of our trip, we just have to make one last detour over the mountains. Instead of taking the easy route through the valley, via Rawang, we choose the B23 through Selangor State Park. One last turn through the jungle, then we find ourselves back in the big city again.

AWAS

THE SOUTH LOOP

Rennfahrer-Gefühl: zweiter Versuch einer perfekten Linie. Du kennst die Kurven aus der Runde vorher, aber nun wirst du sie besser erwischen. Endgültig. Ganz großes Gefühl. Die Vorfreude ist also riesengroß – auch wenn wir nur ein zweites Mal aus Kuala Lumpur nach Norden hinausfahren. Die schwingenden Kurven hinauf in die Genting Highlands. Vorbei an den Batu-Höhlen, raus aus der Stadt, hoch zur Grenze der Bundesstaaten Selangor und Pahang. Hier sind wir auf unserer ersten Etappe auf den North Loop abgebogen, aber heute geht es nach diesen ersten bekannten Kilometern weiter nach Osten.

Der Highway E8 surft mit seinen vier Spuren elegant dahin, legt harmonische Schwünge ins Hügelland, aber wir nehmen seine freundliche Einladung nicht an. In direkter Nachbarschaft presst sich schließlich die 68 durchs Tal, ein winziges Asphaltband mit Tanzbeinen: Einlenken, Auslenken, Beschleunigen, Bremsen – pulsierend und derbe sammelt diese kleine Straße ihre Kilometer. Umtanzt dabei die Schnellstraße auf ihren Brückenpfeilern, ihrer mächtigen Trasse, mit leichten Beinen. Bis Bentong geht das so, dann erst lassen wir locker. Wechseln nun doch auf die große Bahn, denn die ist auf unserer Route weiter nach Osten ab hier die eindeutig beste Option. Selbstbewusst und stetig strebt sie auf Karak zu, dreht dann bei und schiebt nun geradeaus durch die Ebene zwischen Karak und Lanchang. Bei Temerloh strebt von Norden der Sungai Pahang heran, ein schlam-

That racing feeling: a second attempt at a perfect line. You know the corners from the previous lap, but you'll negotiate them better this time around. Finally. What a great feeling. The anticipation is huge – although this is only our second time driving north out of Kuala Lumpur. We climb the dynamic curves up into the Genting Highlands, past the Batu Caves, out of town, as far as the border of Selangor and Pahang states. Here we turned onto the northern loop the first time around, but this time, after the first few familiar kilometers, we head further east.

The E8 highway surfs elegantly along on four lanes, inviting us to enjoy its harmonious curves through the hill country, but we have other things on our mind. Nearby, Route 68 finally pushes its way insistently through the valley, a tiny strip of asphalt with its dancing shoes on: turn in, turn out, accelerate, brake – pulsating and rough, this little road covers an impressive distance. In sprightly fashion it circumnavigates the expressway with its raised pillars and continues in similar style as far as Bentong, where we can finally relax. We then switch to the main road as the best option for our continued journey east. Steady and consistent, it presses on towards Karak where it turns and cuts a straight path through the plain between Karak and Lanchang. At Temerloh, the Sungai Pahang approaches from the north, a muddy river that bends in a wide arc, then winds with us to the east. Palm oil plantations fill the

Ein dramatischer Tempowechsel ist das, die Straße scheint regelrecht aus ihrem Halbschlaf der letzten, vielen Kilometer zu erwachen, sie sprintet unternehmungslustig davon. Schmiegt sich in die sanften Wellen des Geländes, groovt, swingt, zieht an, lässt wieder locker.

It's a dramatic change of pace, the road seems to be waking up from the half-sleep of the last few kilometers and sprints away adventurously. It settles into the gentle waves of the terrain, grooving, swinging, drawing you in, then letting go again.

miger Fluss, der in großem Bogen beidreht, sich dann mit uns nach Osten windet. Palmöl-Plantagen füllen das Land, scheinen jeden Quadratmeter erobern zu wollen, reihen sich treppenförmig auf kleinen Hügeln, füllen Täler und Senken, ziehen bis zum Horizont. Hinter Maran findet aber auch das ein Ende, mächtige Tropenbäume in der Umklammerung von Schlingpflanzen verfolgen uns nun in lichten Rudeln. Bei Gambang verlassen wir die E8, stolpern mit müden Beinen noch einige Kilometer weiter, bis wir bei der großen Stadt Pahang angekommen sind. Weiter im Süden liegt die

landscape, seemingly determined to conquer every square meter, lining up in steps on small hills, infiltrating valleys and hollows and stretching to the horizon. Beyond Maran, however, the plantations also come to an end and sparse clusters of mighty creeper-clad tropical trees now pursue us.

We leave the E8 at Gambang, stumble a few more kilometers onwards on tired legs, until we arrive at the big city of Pahang. Further south is the mouth of the Sungai Pahang on the South China Sea. We drive to there, sidling up to the coast on the

Mündung des Sungai Pahang ins Südchinesische Meer, bis hierher fahren wir noch, schleichen uns auf der „Laluan Persekutuan 3" an die Küste heran und legen dann eine erste Pause ein. Mangroven-Sümpfe ziehen sich am Meer entlang, die Küste ist gesäumt von weißen Sandstränden. Als AH18 gleitet die Straße nun nach Süden, immer weiter dem Band aus Brandung und nachgelagerten Feuchtgebieten folgend. Große Städte sind an dieser Küste kaum vorhanden, aber kleine Siedlungen reihen sich in der Ebene auf, das Leben trägt Flip-Flops und T-Shirt. Gewundene Flüsse schlingern aus dem Landesinneren daher, geben schüchtern ihr braungrünes Wasser an den Ozean ab. Als sedimentreiche Wolke wabert es noch ein paar hundert Meter weit hinaus ins Meer, dann wird es verschlungen vom Pazifik.

Die ruhige Geradeausfahrt dauert Stunden. Als wir dann bei unserem südöstlichen Wendepunkt bei Mersing angekommen sind, haben wir nahezu so viele Kilometer zurückgelegt, wie auf der vorherigen Überquerung der malaiischen Halbinsel herüber aus Kuala Lumpur an die Ostküste. Und jetzt haben wir genug vom sanften Dahinstreichen unter Palmwedeln am Meer, hinter der kleinen Siedlung Jemaluang biegen wir nach rechts ab, in Richtung Westen. Ein dramatischer Tempowechsel ist das, die Straße scheint regelrecht aus ihrem Halbschlaf der letzten, vielen Kilometer zu erwachen, sie sprintet unternehmungslustig davon. Schmiegt sich in die sanften Wellen des Geländes, groovt, swingt, zieht an, lässt wieder locker.

Mal dampft sie mit breiter Brust dahin, weist den umgebenden Dschungel schroff in seine Schranken. Dann scheint sie ihren Übermut zu verlieren und tappst zurückhaltend dahin, während der Urwald auf sie eindringt. Der breitet sich mittlerweile rund um uns meilenweit aus, konturloses,

"Laluan Persekutuan 3" and then take a first break. Mangrove swamps stretch along the sea, the coast lined with white sandy beaches. As it becomes the AH18, the road now glides south, continuing to follow the silken ribbon of surf and wetlands downstream.

There are very few big cities on this coast, but small settlements line the plain. Life here is all about flip-flops and T-shirts. Winding rivers lurch towards the sea, shyly pouring their brown-green waters into the receiving ocean. It drifts a few hundred meters further out into the briny as a sediment-rich cloud, before being swallowed up by the Pacific. The quiet, straight drive takes several hours. When we then arrived at our south-east turning point at Mersing, we had covered almost as many kilometers as on the previous crossing of the Malay Peninsula from Kuala Lumpur to the east coast.

By now we've had enough of gently swaying palm fronds and sea air, so, just beyond the small settlement of Jemaluang we turn right, heading west. It's a dramatic change of pace, the road seems to be waking up from the half-sleep of the last few kilometers and sprints away adventurously. It settles into the gentle waves of the terrain, grooving, swinging, drawing you in, then letting go again. Sometimes it steams along proudly with its chest puffed up, sternly putting the surrounding jungle in its place. It then seems to lose its exuberance and gropes along tentatively as the jungle pushes ever closer. It is now spreading for miles around us, featureless, green growth, complete wilderness, quite beautiful. The land is moist and spongy, continuously cleared drainage ditches keep the road free from invasion by the swampy landscape. Eventually the country opens up again, fields begin to spread expansively and the road dawdles

Das Land ist feucht und schwammig, stetig gezogene Entwässerungsgräben halten den Straßendamm vom nagenden Zahn der Sumpflandschaft frei.

The land is moist and spongy, continuously cleared drainage ditches keep the road free from invasion by the swampy landscape.

grünes Wuchern, völlige Wildheit, wunderschön. Das Land ist feucht und schwammig, stetig gezogene Entwässerungsgräben halten den Straßendamm vom nagenden Zahn der Sumpflandschaft frei.

Irgendwann öffnet sich das Land wieder, Felder breiten sich aus, die Straße trödelt geradeaus dahin. Aber das geht nicht lange so, dann stellen sich vor Kluang erneut Hügel in unseren Weg, hier drehen wir nach Norden ab. Ziehen einen weiten Bogen bis Paloh, schlagen uns dann unaufhörlich kurvend bis nach Yong Peng weiter durchs Land. Unser Ziel, die Hafenstadt Malakka an der Westküste, ist nun noch etwas über 100 Kilometer entfernt – ein Klacks, nach dieser hypnotischen Fahrt. Entgeistert streunen wir unter kolonialen Fassaden durch die historische Altstadt, schauen dem bunten Treiben zu, verstehen die Welt nicht mehr, die für so viele Kilometer einfach nur ein schmales Band aus Asphalt war und nun schillert wie ein Regenbogen. Morgen fahren wir hinauf nach Kuala Lumpur, an den Anfang unserer Reise. Morgen.

along on a straight path. However, this doesn't last long, as there are more hills in our way before we reach Kluang, where we turn north. We make a wide arc toward Paloh, then continue to wend our way through the country to Yong Peng. Our destination, the port city of Malacca on the west coast, is now just over 100 kilometers away – easy-peasy after this hypnotic drive. Stunned, we wander through the historic old town with its colonial facades, watching the hustle and bustle.

We have lost all understanding the world that was just a narrow band of asphalt for so many kilometers and now shimmers before us like a rainbow. Tomorrow we will drive up to Kuala Lumpur to the start of our journey. But that's for tomorrow.

BAC KST AGE

CURVES landet in Malaysia. Auf einem fremden Planeten. Weit weg von Munich, Germany, unserem Hauptquartier. Oder sind wir der fremde Planet, mit unseren Alpenpässen, der Jahresdurchschnittstemperatur von 10 Grad, einer durchschnittlichen Luftfeuchte von 75 Prozent? Und ist Malaysia normal? Mit Dschungel und Ozeanen, über 28 Grad im Schnitt und knapp 90% triefender Luftfeuchte? – Kann man so oder so sehen. Sicher ist aber, dass CURVES in Malaysia nicht ohne die warme Umarmung eines örtlichen Empfangskomitees gelandet wäre. Nicht so. Nicht so reibungslos, organisch, begeistert. – Wir hatten gerade noch viele hundert Kilometer auf deutschen Straßen hinter uns, in diesem alten, komplizierten und wunderschönen Land, das wir Zuhause nennen, und fanden uns plötzlich in Kuala Lumpur wieder. On the bright side of the moon. Süßer Schock. Innere Uhr auf zu früh, frei drehende Kompassnadel. Am anderen Ende der Welt, Lichtjahre entfernt vom normalen CURVES-Lebensgefühl – was auch immer normal ist.

In so einer Situation brauchst du jemanden, der dich an die Hand nimmt. Dir den Puls fühlt. Dich einfach mit hinein nimmt, in einen fremdartigen Wahnsinn, der sich dann, ein paar Augenblicke später, schon anfühlt, als sei man angekommen. Und das sind wir tatsächlich. CURVES in Malaysia. Wenn sich dann der Ruhepuls bei seidiger Leerlaufdrehzahl einpendelt, du diese andere Realität einer Welt in einer fremden Zeitzone, auf einem anderen Breiten- und Längengrad neugierig beäugst, während

CURVES takes to the road in Malaysia. It feels like an alien planet, eons away from our headquarters in Munich, Germany. But maybe we are the alien planet, with our Alpine passes, annual average temperature of 10 degrees, average humidity of 75 percent. But maybe Malaysia is normal, with its jungle and oceans, average temperatures of over 28 degrees and almost 90% humidity. – You could argue one way or the other.

What is certain, however, is that CURVES would not have ventured to Malaysia without the warm reception afforded by a local welcoming committee. It simply wouldn't have happened, or at least not as smoothly and organically, without their enthusiastic support. – We had no sooner covered many hundreds of kilometers on German roads in this old, complicated and beautiful country we call home when we suddenly found ourselves in Kuala Lumpur. On the bright side of the moon. This was a sweet shock to the system. Our internal clock went haywire, as did any sense of direction. We were on the other side of the world, light years away from the normal CURVES way of life – whatever normal actually means.

In a situation like this, you need someone who will hold your hand and take your pulse. Someone to guide you gently into a strangely crazy world which, just a few moments later, already feels as if you've arrived. And indeed we have. CURVES has made it to Malaysia. Once your resting heart rate levels off at a smooth idle speed, you start to take stock of this other reality in a foreign time

du hinter einem Porsche Speedster eine schmale Asphaltpiste in einen südostasiatischen Urwald hinabtrudelst, während links und rechts ein magischer Dschungel heranschwappt, entdeckst du verwundert, dass das ein Moment ist, der dir seltsam vertraut vorkommt. Du kennst ihn. Er funktioniert in Munich, Germany, wie in Kuala Lumpur, Malaysia, und überall sonst. Freude, heißt dieser Moment. Strahlende Freude.

Und Lebenslust. Entdecken, was kommt, im nächsten Atemzug. Die Porsche-Community feiert das auf der ganzen Welt, wir wussten das natürlich längst, aber wundern uns immer noch, wenn wir über dieses universelle Freuen stolpern. So vergesslich sind wir. Und deshalb: Danke. Danke an Porsche Asia Pacific für die famose Unterstützung, für die Gastfreundschaft, fürs Möglichmachen.

Danke an Porsche Malaysia, den großartigen Winston, die gesamte Kuala-Lumpur-Crew. Und an den Porsche Club Malaysia. Ein herzhaftes „Hossa" geht raus an die „911 Rebels", High Five an die „Renndrive"-Freunde, die aus Thailand nach Malaysia heruntergefahren sind, um erneut ein paar Kilometer Straße mit uns zu teilen. Danke für all die Freundschaft und Begeisterung, das Zuhausesein am Ende unserer Welt. Danke für die Wildheit, die Schönheit, die Farben. Danke dass ihr uns zeigt, was Soulful Driving heißt.

zone, on a different latitude and longitude, as you plunge down a narrow asphalt track into a Southeast Asian jungle behind a Porsche Speedster, while to the left and right a magical jungle closes in around you. You realize with amazement that this is a moment that seems strangely familiar to you.

You know it well. It is the same whether you're in Munich, Germany, in Kuala Lumpur, Malaysia, or anywhere else. This moment is called joy. Pure, radiant joy. A genuine lust for life. Discovering what's coming as you take your next breath. The Porsche community celebrates this feeling all over the world. Of course we have known this for a long time, but we are still surprised when we stumble across this universal rejoicing. That's an indication of how forgetful we are. So, we need to say some thank you's. Thanks to Porsche Asia Pacific for their incredible support and hospitality and for making this happen. Thanks to Porsche Malaysia, the brilliant Winston and the entire Kuala Lumpur crew. Thanks also to Porsche Club Malaysia. Also a hearty shout-out to the "911 Rebels", a high five to our "Renndrive" friends, who drove down from Thailand to Malyasia to spend more time with us on the road. Thanks for all your friendship and enthusiasm and for making us feel at home at the end of our world. Thanks for the wild times, the beauty and the colors. Thank you for showing us what Soulful Driving really means.

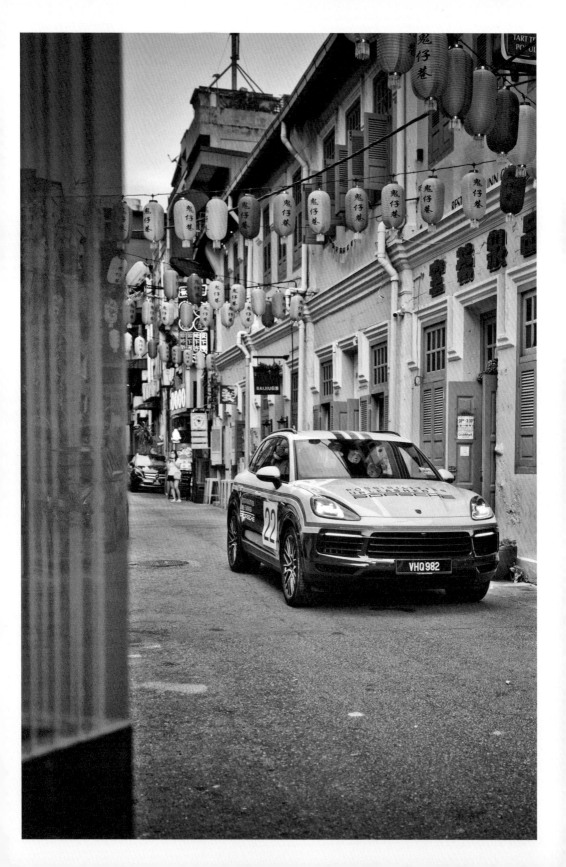

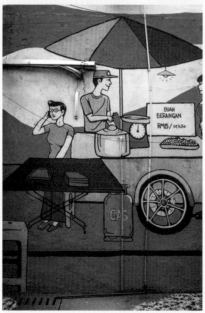

DANK AN / THANKS TO PHILIPP HEITSCH, BEN WINTER, MICHAEL DORN, MICHAELA BOGNER, RALF VOGL • THE PAP TEAM • PORSCHE MALAYSIA TEAM • WINSTON AND YANNICK • 911 REBELS: REMUS CHANG SURPREMUS • KAMALESHWARAN RAGAVAN • JIGGEE JON • SPENCER CYRUS MEHTA • LAY HC • RAJAY SINGH AND MOTORSPORT PLAYGROUND • THE RENNDRIVE CREW AND THE MECHANICS • TENN, OUU, SUTHIDEJ, A.GT, HUMPHREY, NICK AND KHUN BOBBY • PORSCHE CLUB MALAYSIA • SPECIAL THANKS: RECSTORM PICTURES: JOHN CHONG • JAY CHUA • SAMUEL LOW // AOT TRAVEL TEAM

Porsche Cayenne
Fuel consumption combined: 9.2l/100km
CO2 emissions: 209g/km

IMPRESSUM / IMPRINT

HERAUSGEBER/
PUBLISHER: CURVES MAGAZIN
THIERSCHSTRASSE 25
D-80538 MÜNCHEN
VERANTWORTLICH FÜR
DEN HERAUSGEBER/
RESPONSIBLE FOR
PUBLICATION:
STEFAN BOGNER
KONZEPT/CONCEPT:
STEFAN BOGNER
THIERSCHSTRASSE 25
D-80538 MÜNCHEN

DELIUS KLASING
CORPORATE PUBLISHING
SIEKERWALL 21
D-33602 BIELEFELD
REDAKTION/
EDITORIAL CONTENT:
STEFAN BOGNER
BEN WINTER

ART DIRECTION, LAYOUT,
FOTOS/ART DIRECTION,
LAYOUT, PHOTOS:
STEFAN BOGNER

MAKING OF PHOTOS:
PHILLIPP HEITSCH
TEXT/TEXT: BEN WINTER
TEXT INTRO/TEXT
INTRO: BEN WINTER

MOTIVAUSARBEITUNG
LITHOGRAPHIE/SATZ/
POST-PRODUCTION,
LITHOGRAPHY/
SETTING:
MICHAEL DORN

ÜBERSETZUNG/TRANSLA-
TION JAMES O'NEILL

PRODUKTIONSLEITUNG/
PRODUCTION MANAGE-
MENT: AXEL GERBER

DRUCK/PRINT:
DRUCKEREI VOGL

1. AUFLAGE/1ST EDITION:
ISBN: 978-3-667-12733-4

AUSGEZEICHNET MIT / AWARDED WITH

CURVES AUSGABEN / OTHER ISSUES OF CURVES

PYRENÄEN / PYRENEES — Im Handel erhältlich/Available in stores
ÖSTERREICH / AUSTRIA — Im Handel erhältlich/Available in stores
SCHWEIZ / SWITZERLAND — Im Handel erhältlich/Available in stores
SCHOTTLAND / SCOTLAND — Im Handel erhältlich/Available in stores
FRANKREICH / FRANCE — Im Handel erhältlich/Available in stores
USA · KALIFORNIEN / USA · CALIFORNIA — Im Handel erhältlich/Available in stores
NORDITALIEN / NORTHERN ITALY — Im Handel erhältlich/Available in stores
ISLAND / ICELAND — Im Handel erhältlich/Available in stores

NORWEGEN / NORWAY — Im Handel erhältlich/Available in stores
SPANIEN · MALLORCA / SPAIN · MALLORCA — Im Handel erhältlich/Available in stores
USA · COLORADO/UTAH / USA · COLORADO/UTAH — Im Handel erhältlich/Available in stores
THAILAND / THAILAND — Im Handel erhältlich/Available in stores
SÜDDEUTSCHLAND / SOUTHERN GERMANY — Im Handel erhältlich/Available in stores
PORTUGAL / PORTUGAL — Im Handel erhältlich/Available in stores
SIZILIEN / SICILY — Im Handel erhältlich/Available in stores
OSTDEUTSCHLAND / EASTERN GERMANY — Im Handel erhältlich/Available in stores